Angels Whisper Series

Angels Whisper
The Nativity Story

Where Christmas Came From

Written by: Ray McClendon

Illustrated by: Russell Oliviera

This book is a work of non-fiction. Unless otherwise noted, the author and the publisher make no explicit guarantees as to the accuracy of the information contained in this book and in some cases, names of people and places have been altered to protect their privacy.

Scripture taken from the New King James Version®. Copyright © 1982 by Thomas Nelson. Used by permission. All rights reserved.

Scripture quotations marked (NLT) are taken from the Holy Bible, New Living Translation, copyright ©1996, 2004, 2015

Artist: Russell Oliviera
Angels Whisper Series Logo: Deb Hoeffner

WestBow Press books may be ordered through booksellers or by contacting:

WestBow Press
A Division of Thomas Nelson & Zondervan
1663 Liberty Drive
Bloomington, IN 47403
www.westbowpress.com
1 (866) 928-1240

Because of the dynamic nature of the Internet, any web addresses or links contained in this book may have changed since publication and may no longer be valid. The views expressed in this work are solely those of the author and do not necessarily reflect the views of the publisher, and the publisher hereby disclaims any responsibility for them.

Any people depicted in stock imagery provided by Getty Images are models, and such images are being used for illustrative purposes only.
Certain stock imagery © Getty Images.

ISBN: 978-1-9736-4673-0 (sc)
ISBN: 978-1-9736-4674-7 (e)

Library of Congress Control Number: 2018914023

Print information available on the last page.

WestBow Press rev. date: 12/5/2018

WESTBOW
PRESS®
A DIVISION OF THOMAS NELSON
& ZONDERVAN

This book is dedicated to my high school sweetheart.

God first saved me in and through the person of Jesus.

He has since been saving me for the last 42 years

through my loving and faithful wife, Linda.

It's been two thousand years or so,

since Jesus came to earth.

Two thousand years have come and gone,

since our dear Savior's birth.

And this old **WORLD** e'er since that day,

has never been the same.

Nor, will it ever be again…

…since Jesus came.

The beginning of the Gospel, the birth of God's dear son.
Gabriel came to Mary and said, "Greetings, favored one!"[A]
He told her do not be afraid, t'was a blessing through and through.
That she'd conceive and bear a son, and name Him Jesus too."

[A] Luke 1:28, New Revised Standard Version

But Mary asked, "How can this be, since I'm a virgin still ?"
The angel told her she'd conceive, according to His will.
Assuring her God's promises always would prevail.
The Angel said, "For the word of God will never fail."[B]
So Mary glorified the Lord, her spirit did rejoice.
That Israel's God was mindful of His humble servant's voice.
That generations from now on, would call her Blessed One,
for all the Holy, Mighty God had mercifully done.

[B] Luke 1:37, New Living Translation

When Joseph heard
about the child,
he was upset, of course!
But thought it best for everyone,
to quietly divorce. For he was
faithful to the Law…

…yet wanted no disgrace;
for, he cared about
his Mary and his
Mary saving face.

While Joseph slept an angel spoke, who wanted him to hear it.
"...the child who has been conceived in her, is of the Holy Spirit."[c]
Joseph named Him Jesus for he would save us from our sin.
And he awoke in faith that morn, peaceful deep within.

[c] Matthew 1:20, New American Standard

He would also be **Immanuel—God with us**—in our night.

So said the Prophets long ago, He'd fill the world with light.

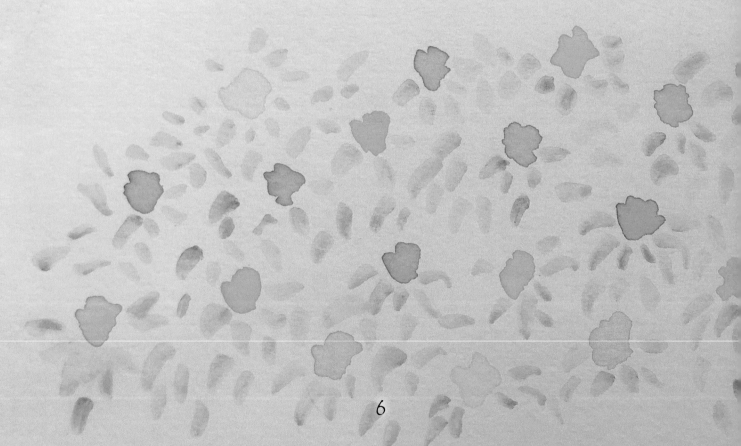

Then Joseph, son of David,
took Mary for his wife.
But she remained a virgin,
'til Jesus was born to life.

Then Caesar sent an order to all nations under Rome,
that families paying taxes must go register back home.

So Joseph left from Nazareth and returned to Bethlehem,
along with Mary—pregnant still—the Lord was blessing them.

With all the people
coming home, there
was no place to stay.
The inn they
tried had no
more rooms—
just a barn and
beds of hay.

There, Mary felt her labor pains.
T'was time for Jesus' birth.
She wrapped her babe in strips
of cloth, Lord of heaven and earth!

Who would have thought the Son
of God would be so meek, so mild,
that He would come to all of us,
a poor, woodworker's child.

Some shepherds in the fields nearby,
were watching sheep at night.
An angel came (which
frightened them!),
in glory, shining bright !
"Do not be afraid..."
he said, "...I am
bringing you
good news..."[D]

He told them of Messiah's birth, the Savior of the Jews!

Christ the Lord—the Anointed One—will be Lord of all.

The babe was wrapped in swaddling cloths, lying in a stall.

A heavenly choir of angels then,
gathered 'round to praise...

14

...and glorify the God of all,
with happy, joyful phrase!

15

The shepherds said, "Now we must go,
to see this wondrous thing...

...that God has said has happened there,
the birth of Israel's King!"

The shepherds hurried quickly there and found the Christ-child king. Lying in a manger oh what a wondrous thing!

They spoke of all the angels said would set this child apart. Mary treasured all these things deep down inside her heart.

19

When the boy was eight days old,

the name that Joseph gave,

was the name the angel gave to him...

... J E S U S, God will save!

Three wise men saw the shining star—came through Jerusalem, looking for the infant King, that they might worship him.

From afar they
followed the star,
to where Jesus
and Mary were.

Then, filled with awe they gave him gifts...

It's been two thousand years or so,

since Jesus came to earth.

Two thousand years have come and gone,

since our dear Savior's birth.

And this old **HEART** e'er since that day,

has never been the same.

Nor, will it ever be again…

…since Jesus came.

"For there is born to you this day
in the city of David a Savior,
who is Christ the Lord.
And this will be the sign to you.
You will find a Babe wrapped in
swaddling cloths, lying in a manger."
Suddenly, there was with the angel
a multitude of the heavenly
host, praising God and saying,
"Glory to God in the highest, and on
earth peace, goodwill toward men!"

Luke 2:11–14
NKJV

Printed in the United States
By Bookmasters